Exploring public views

Sophie Tolmie

Exploring public views and perceptions of facial disfigurement

I don't like your face!'- Exploring public views and perceptions of facial disfigurement: a qualitative investigation

VDM Verlag Dr. Müller

Impressum/Imprint (nur für Deutschland/ only for Germany)
Bibliografische Information der Deutschen Nationalbibliothek: Die Deutsche Nationalbibliothek verzeichnet diese Publikation in der Deutschen Nationalbibliografie; detaillierte bibliografische Daten sind im Internet über http://dnb.d-nb.de abrufbar.

Alle in diesem Buch genannten Marken und Produktnamen unterliegen warenzeichen-, marken- oder patentrechtlichem Schutz bzw. sind Warenzeichen oder eingetragene Warenzeichen der jeweiligen Inhaber. Die Wiedergabe von Marken, Produktnamen, Gebrauchsnamen, Handelsnamen, Warenbezeichnungen u.s.w. in diesem Werk berechtigt auch ohne besondere Kennzeichnung nicht zu der Annahme, dass solche Namen im Sinne der Warenzeichen- und Markenschutzgesetzgebung als frei zu betrachten wären und daher von jedermann benutzt werden dürften.

Coverbild: www.ingimage.com

Verlag: VDM Verlag Dr. Müller GmbH & Co. KG
Dudweiler Landstr. 99, 66123 Saarbrücken, Deutschland
Telefon +49 681 9100-698, Telefax +49 681 9100-988
Email: info@vdm-verlag.de

Herstellung in Deutschland:
Schaltungsdienst Lange o.H.G., Berlin
Books on Demand GmbH, Norderstedt
Reha GmbH, Saarbrücken
Amazon Distribution GmbH, Leipzig
ISBN: 978-3-639-32243-9

Imprint (only for USA, GB)
Bibliographic information published by the Deutsche Nationalbibliothek: The Deutsche Nationalbibliothek lists this publication in the Deutsche Nationalbibliografie; detailed bibliographic data are available in the Internet at http://dnb.d-nb.de.

Any brand names and product names mentioned in this book are subject to trademark, brand or patent protection and are trademarks or registered trademarks of their respective holders. The use of brand names, product names, common names, trade names, product descriptions etc. even without a particular marking in this works is in no way to be construed to mean that such names may be regarded as unrestricted in respect of trademark and brand protection legislation and could thus be used by anyone.

Cover image: www.ingimage.com

Publisher: VDM Verlag Dr. Müller GmbH & Co. KG
Dudweiler Landstr. 99, 66123 Saarbrücken, Germany
Phone +49 681 9100-698, Fax +49 681 9100-988
Email: info@vdm-publishing.com

Printed in the U.S.A.
Printed in the U.K. by (see last page)
ISBN: 978-3-639-32243-9

Copyright © 2011 by the author and VDM Verlag Dr. Müller GmbH & Co. KG
and licensors
All rights reserved. Saarbrücken 2011

Queen Margaret University
EDINBURGH

TITLE- *'I don't like your face!'* - Exploring public views and perceptions of facial disfigurement: a qualitative investigation.

BY *Sophie Tolmie/ 06004308*

DISSERTATION SUBMITTED IN PARTIAL FULFILMENT OF THE REQUIREMENTS FOR THE DEGREE OF BACHELOR OF ARTS WITH HONOURS IN PSYCHOLOGY.

*'Should I destroy my eyes?
So I cannot see in yours.
That horror and pity you try to hide-
Long ago your mother told you it isn't
Polite to stare at people who are 'different';
And so you are embarrassed...-even you.
Or shall I destroy your eyes?
Then only my voice will speak to you-
Beyond the inessentials we will meet for the first time.'*

(Trust, 1986;p.23)

Text word count 10900 (may be 10 words difference either way)

Acknowledgments

Firstly, I would like to gratefully acknowledge the help and support of my supervisor, Zoe Chouliara, thank you for your assistance.

Secondly, I would like to thank my dad's friend Thom, for his helpful comments on my first draft. I would also like to thank my parents for your love and support during this stressful year!

Contents	Page
Abstract	5
Chapter 1- *introduction and literature review*	6-15
Chapter 2- *Methodology*	15-19
Chapter 3 –*Results*	20-31
Chapter 4 –*Discussion*	32-42
References	43-48
Appendix 1- *Information sheet*	49-50
Appendix 2 *Consent from*	51-52
Appendix 3- *Debriefing sheet*	53
Appendix 4- *Interview schedule*	54
Appendix 5- *Images 1-3.*	55-57

Abstract

One in eleven people in the United Kingdom have a significant disfigurement to their face (Changing Faces, 2007, unpublished). Those with a facial disfigurement are often victims of prejudice and stigmatisation, there is however lack of understanding of why this occurs. This research aims to explore public views' and perceptions of facial disfigurement. Semi-structured interviews were carried out on six participants. As a result of extensive Interpretative Phenomenological Analysis, 4 super- ordinate themes emerged from the data, 1)different from normal, 2)social awkwardness,3) perceived negative impact on the lives of those with a disfigurement and 4) society and disfigurement. These themes will be discussed in association to previous findings in research, and possible future directions for research will be highlighted.

Chapter 1
Introduction and literature review

In February of this year, the BBC received a number of complaints from parents concerning a children's presenter who has a disfigurement. They were concerned that this woman's disfigurement would scare their children, and may cause them distress. This example highlights contemporary evidence of society's ignorance and misunderstanding of disfigurement.

' *The word 'disfigurement' is used to describe the aesthetic effects of a mark, rash, scar or skin graft on a person's skin or an asymmetry or paralysis to their face or body. Disfigurement can affect anyone and any time, at any age, from any ethnic group whether from birth, accident, disease or the aftermath of surgery*' (Changing Faces, 2009).

This definition '*depends on an interaction between social norms and individual attitudes and values*' (Thomson, 2001; p. 664). It is hard to pin point as there are a number of causes of facial disfigurement, and what some might consider a disfigurement, may not be perceived in the same way by another individual(Harcourt & Rumsey, 2008). Disfigurement has been classified as a disability under the Disability Discrimination Act of 1995; therefore, it is now illegal to discriminate on the grounds of disfigurement or appearance.

It is estimated by research carried out by Changing Faces in 2007(unpublished), that one in eleven have a significant disfigurement to their face and over 400,000 are anticipated to acquire a facial disfigurement, in the period of a year. These figures demonstrate the huge extent of facial disfigurement in the British population, although these figures are not exact, they are believed to be the most accurate to date (Changing faces, 2009). The sheer prevalence of facial disfigurement highlights the importance for education and research into the phenomenon. In addition, Facial disfigurement is a particularly important form of disfigurement, as disfigurements that are exposed are perceived to be most severe, and have the largest psychological impact (Yanik et al., 2004).

Use of language and definitions.

Although this research will use the word disfigurement, it is recognised that this definition holds negative connotations (Rumsey & Harcourt, 2003). It has been used throughout this project as Changing Faces says it is a concise and common definition that is used in society, and the word brings to mind a universal understanding of the phenomenon (Changing Faces, 2009; Rumsey & Harcourt, 2003).

1:2 Cultural and historical aspects of facial disfigurement

As a society, we have had a long-standing obsession with our appearance throughout history (see Rumsey & Harcourt, 2005 for a review). Research has stated that attractiveness holds huge advantages for individuals (Eagley et al., 1991). Dion, Berschfield and Walster (1972) stated that this stereotype has caused society to perceive more 'attractive' people as more successful, to have a better quality of life, and to have better personalities and relationships. This social stereotype is reinforced in many areas of society. Roche (2008) has written about 'The Metaphor of Facial Disfigurement', he describes how facial disfigurement is used as a metaphor in films to depict 'evilness', for example '*The Nightmare on Elm Street*'. McGouther,(1997) points out that if films were portraying race in the same way they portray 'ugliness', they could face legal action. Furthermore, due to the power the media has on standards of beauty, the continuing use of images of flawless models will promote this stereotype. As those with a disfigurement are often thought to be 'unclean' due to their facial disfigurement, Partridge (1990) points out the danger of advertising companies using images of blemish free and 'perfect' individuals on society's attitude towards disfigurement.

The face itself holds further significance for communication, social interaction and for individual identity (Elks, 1990;Rumsey, 2004; Tebble et al., 2006). Furthermore, 'Psychological research confirms that our face plays a central role in the way we think and feel about ourselves; our image is affected by the smallest spot, especially if we think other people will make judgements about us because of it' Dr Nicola Rumsey. (Cited in Partridge, 1996).

Disfigurement is largely a socially defined phenomena (Elks, 1990). After World War II, Partridge (1990) has pointed out that those who were left with a facial disfigurement due to war injuries were *'all accorded public respect without question'* (p.120); this suggests that situational factors may contribute to how the public respond to facial disfigurement. Researchers have suggested that our view of disfigurement is in line with our cultural values; disfigurements on younger females are viewed to have a larger impact than those on older males, and as a culture we value attractiveness in young females, further suggesting our view towards facial disfigurement is culturally defined (Gardiner et al., 2008). The history of disfigurement further highlights the negative view towards it as a culturally created prejudice. There is evidence to suggest that the ancient Egyptians viewed disfigurement as a positive entity and they widely accepted disfigurement (Sullivan, 2001). However, the ancient Greeks had an opposing view of disfigurement, which Garland (1995) suggested in his writings is the origins of modern day prejudice. e.g., Plato expressed the view that the states of the outer body 'was important for the ascent of the soul' (Sullivan, 2001; p. 263). This reflects many of today's ideas surrounding disfigurement. Throughout history, art has depicted disfigurement as a metaphor for evilness and criminality (Rumsey & Harcourt, 2005). Johann Caspar, in the late 18 century, stated in his writings that 'the morally worst, the most deformed' (cited in Sullivan, 2001). These examples portray society's long held prejudices and inaccurate beliefs surrounding facial disfigurement, demonstrating how it has been socially defined.

Cash (1990) noted that the difficulties experienced by those with a facial disfigurement have followed two lines of related enquiries; 'the view from the outside', namely, how the facial disfigurement affects public perceptions and social encounters. The second line is 'the view from the inside', which is the effect of the facial disfigurement on the individual personally; their self concept, confidence and quality of life.

1.3 *'View from the outside'- public reactions and views of facial disfigurement*
Definitions

The word prejudice will be used in the sense described by Allport (1954);

'prejudice is an antipathy based upon a faulty and inflexible generalization. It may be felt or expressed. It may be directed toward a group as a whole, or toward an individual because he is a member of that group' (Allport, 1954:p. 9).

In addition, the word stigmatisation will be used in the sense that Goffman (1963) used it;

Stigma is the situation of the individual who is disqualified from full social acceptance....he is thus reduced in our minds from a whole and usual person to a tainted, discounted one" (Goffman, 1963: 3).

The public discrimination and stigmatisation of facial disfigurement is well documented. This success of this research has been assisted by the study of facial disfigurement as a single concept, rather than a health condition (Clarke, 1999). In an on-going Implicit Attitude Test (IAT), over 90% of individuals had an unconscious prejudice towards facial disfigurement (Changing Faces, 2008;unpublished). The study was carried out to reveal if the anecdotal evidence, such as stares, teasing and taunting, reported by those with a facial disfigurement, was correct. It is thought that identifying these 'unconscious' feelings is very important in psychology as many people report what they feel is sociably desirable, rather than the truth. Even though they had claimed that they had no prejudice towards people with a facial disfigurement, they saw them as less attractive, as having a lower quality of life, being lower in success and short of social skills. This prejudice was present irrespective of age, gender or socioeconomic status. Furthermore, those with a disfigurement are often victim to aggression, teased, and stared at (Changing faces, 2000; Gerrard, 1991; Lansdown et al., 1997; Noar, 1991). In addition, they often experience avoidance and rejection (Finlay et al., 1990; Bull & Rumsey, 1988).

Macgregor (1990) undertook a 30-year qualitative investigation into the societal effects that disfigurement had for individuals and found that;

'In an effort to go about their daily affairs they are subject to visual and verbal assaults...(including) naked stares, startle reactions, 'double takes', whispering, remarks, furtive looks, curiosity, personal questions, advice, manifestations of pity and or aversion, laughter, ridicule, and outright avoidance.' (Macgregor, 1990).

In the 1980's and 1990s a series of studies researched facial disfigurement as a distinct entity. Rumsey, Bull and Gahagan (1986) established that members of the public stood further away from an individual when they stood on the side of their disfigurement of when they were on the opposite side. Furthermore, Bull and Houston (1994) found that the public sat further away from individuals with a disfigurement on an underground. These studies provided the first empirical evidence of avoidance and rejection of those with a facial disfigurement

Ackerman et al. (2009) found that facial disfigurements grasp more interest than 'normal' faces. In addition, first impression's can be affected by the presence of a disfigurement (Partridge, 1996; Thompson, 2001). Jones and Stone (1995) established that it caused more unease in participants than any other kind of physical disability. Furthermore, disfigurement elicited a strong physiological arousal in individuals when they viewed it (Kleck & Strenta, 1985). However many factors may affect an individual's response, including visibility or type of disfigurement (Rumsey & Harcourt,2005; Yamin et al.,2004) location on the face, or gender of the individual (Gardiner et al, 2008). It may also depend on the social skills of the person with the disfigurement (Partridge, 1990). This evidence suggests that although disfigurement will cause a reaction in the observer, situational factors are likely to affect the response elicited. (Greenhouse, 2003; Tevenage & McKay, 1999;Tartaglia et al., 2005).

This negative view and reaction to facial disfigurement has been demonstrated in job recruitment (Greenhouse, 2003; Tevenage & McKay, 1999). There was a significant pessimistic perception towards them by the potential employer, and the presence of a facial disfigurement caused significant negative effect on the participant, for percived job skills and personal qualities. Furthermore, those with a facial disfigurement are more likely to be employed in an industry where they do not have contact with the public, e.g. factory work (Tartaglia et al., 2005).

There is lack of theoretical explanation to explain this view and reaction towards facial disfigurement (Grandfield, Thomson, & Turpin, 2006;Thomson & Kent, 2001). It is vital to be aware of the processes underlying this, in order to make people more aware of their prejudices, as the above ITA demonstrated many people are not aware of their prejudices. Although the cognitive processes behind this prejudice have begun to be explored (Ackerman et al., 2009), the social processes have received little attention: 'Understanding basic cognitive reactions to such individuals is an important step in addressing the stigmatisation they will one day face.' (Ackerman et al., 2009; p.7).

However, the public reactions to facial disfigurement have attracted theories of explanation, e.g. evolutionary (Ackerman et al., 2009; Kurzban & Leary,2001; Park, Faulkner, & Schaller, 2003). The evolutionary models propose that avoidant behaviour of individuals towards those with a facial disfigurement is due to evolved mechanisms, in order to avoid 'disease causing organisms' (Ackerman et al., 2009; p.2). The theory states that facial disfigurements are often cue for contagious disease, and this in turn causes an over bias of avoidant behaviour, as well as negative perceptions towards disfigurement, whether the individuals condition is contagious or not. In contrast, Goffman (1963) suggests that our discrimination towards disfigurement is due to social stigmatisation:

'While a stranger is present before us, evidence can arise of his possessing an attribute that makes him different to others in the category of persons available for him to be, and of a less desirable kind. He is thus reduced in our minds from a whole and unusual person to a tainted, discounted one...such an attribute is called stigma.' (Goffman, 1963; p.12)'

Goffman claims that we have representations of what is socially 'normal', and in turn, we have representations of deviations from this norm. When we encounter someone with a facial disfigurement, they are a deviation from the norm and our perception of their social identity is therefore ruined. This is because we categorise them as a social deviant.

Partridge (1990) has suggest that the stereotypic reactions of people are for 6 reasons which he entitles 'SCARED': sorrow, curiosity, anxiety, repulsion, embarrassment and distress. He suggests that the individual with the disfigurement can do many things to help ease these natural reactions, and that they are inevitable occurrences, which every person with a disfigurement will need experience. He states that observers act the way they do because they are 'scared' of the unknown. However, these theories have been criticised for being too simplistic and that none of these theories alone can explain the complex behaviours of the public towards facial disfigurement and a number of factors will be responsible (Rumsey& Harcourt,

2003). In addition, some accounts may be more suitable, depending on the circumstances (Thomson, 2001).

Partridge (1990) has outlined 4 myths of facial disfigurement: individuals with disfigurement cannot lead a successful and happy life; that surgery can magically 'fix' disfigurement: those individuals' with a disfigurement have no concern with their appearance and that disfigurement can infer our character. He believes that media and film using disfigurement as a metaphor for evil cause these myths. However, these myths have no real foundation (Countinho, 2006).

1.4 Psychological problems caused by facial disfigurement.

Partridge & Pearson (2008) point out that research has pointed towards the psychological difficulties experienced by those with a facial disfigurement having two major, related, causes: interpersonal, caused by difficult social encounters and peoples negative reactions, in turn affecting the individual's social confidence which can cause them to become socially withdrawn. Along with intrapersonal, caused by societal pressures and increasing emphasis on good looks, this can cause individuals with a disfigurement to feel insufficient to the rest of society, leaving them with low self-esteem. This vast pressure on a daily basis, along with the social difficulties, can cause severe anxiety and depression.

Individuals with differing kinds of disfiguring conditions have similar psychological problems. These include, increased levels of anxiety, depression and social avoidance, and often a change in self image, along with feelings of shame (Lansdown et al., 1997; Moss & Rosser, 2008; Rumsey & Harcourt, 2003, 2005). Similarities in psychological problems have been shown across differing conditions, including eye disfigurements (Clarke, et al,2003), burns (Partridge, 1990), systemic sclerosis (Richards et al., 2004), psoriasis, (Schmid-Ott et al, 2007; Wahl et al.,2002), and skin lesions (Schmid-Ott et al, 2003). In addition, in a sample of 250 individuals suffering from a range of disfiguring conditions (Rumsey, Clarke & White, 2003). However, it should be noted there was huge variation in adjustment across these studies (Richards et al., 2004; Rumsey, Clarke & White, 2003; Wahl et al, 2002).

The psychological and social difficulties experienced by individuals with a disfigurement are highly intertwined, related and relevant to one another. Facial disfigurement has been described as a 'social disability' (Macgregor, 1979). Many psychological problems experienced by those with a facial disfigurement are due to experienced stigma (Heason & Kent, 2003. The anxiety problems of those with a facial disfigurement mirror the anxiety and depression seen in social phobia (Newell & Marks, 2000). Furthermore, researchers have found that the difficulties and anxieties experienced by those with a facial disfigurement are explicit to social interaction. In addition, Kent & Keohane, (2001) have shown negative social occurrences reported by those with a facial disfigurement, are correlated with over all well-being in the individual, although these associations were feeble. Cash (1996) has provided a model through which he believes individuals with disfigurements build up a negative body image through our cultural values, which are reinforced by the media, and the value we place on appearance. Negative reactions from society enforce this negative body image, and in turn cause social avoidance and concealment behaviours, and they come to expect negative evaluation from others. This evidence suggests that psychological problems of those with a facial disfigurement are widely social in nature. This demonstrates the importance of understanding social reactions and views towards these individuals.

1.5 Social Intervention

Changing Faces is the leading charity in the area of disfigurement, which aims to combat prejudice and promote face equality throughout the world. They also aim to:

'To raise awareness of implicit attitudes that can result in prejudice and discrimination, encourage people, organisations and the government to tackle such attitudes and make a commitment to face equality and to help everyone learn new ways of thinking and behaving towards people with disfigurements'(taken from the website under *'Why Face Equality Matters'*)

Partridge (1990) has highlighted that the individual with the disfigurement has a role to play in successful social interactions with the public. This is because he believes they can help the observer feel as ease, as if the observer has never encountered anyone with a facial disfigurement, they are likely to feel nervous and uneasy. As a solution, he has recommended social skills training for individuals with a facial disfigurement. Social skills training focuses on strengthening communication skills, and more positive skills for dealing with social situations, helping the individual draw attention away from the disfigurement.

There is evidence to support the usefulness of this intervention. Partridge et al. (1997) found that individuals who were better adjusted had built up a number of differing strategies for social situations, suggesting that the development of social skills could aid in the adjustment process. Furthermore, the experience of being sociallyridiculed can result in appearance anxiety for those with a facial disfigurement; this may result in individuals with a disfigurement being additionally sensitive in social situations, and this may cause them to perceive any negative social experience to be a result of their disfigurement (Cash, 1996; Kent, 2002). This may cause anxiousness and self consciousness, and this social fear in turn causes social avoidance and concealment; which has been demonstrated to cause avoidance and uncertainly in the observer in Partridge's 'feedback' model'(Clark, 1999). By aiding those with a disfigurement to build skills for potentially difficult social encounters, this will aid individuals with a disfigurement.

Many studies have supported the effectiveness of this intervention (Newell,1999;Robison, Rumsey & Partridge,1996; Rumsey et al., 1986). However these studies only can be said to provide limited evidence for its effectiveness (Bessell & Moss, 2007) e.g. Robinson, Rumsey & Partridge (1996) study did not provide a control group. As a result of these limitations, further research is required.

This literature review has highlighted the key areas relevant to the present research. The public prejudice and stigmatisation towards these individuals is well documented. However, as discussed, there is little understanding of the reasons behind public reactions to those with a facial disfigurement; this is a major gap in the research literature. Psychological problems of individuals with a disfigurement are vast, and are widely social in nature, causing this to be a psychosocial issue. Although interventions for these individuals are starting to take place, there is a great need for increased understanding of public views and reactions to facial disfigurement in order to build social and psychological interventions for the public and those with a facial disfigurement, to ease difficulty on both sides.

1.6 Research rationale

The vast majority of research in this area has been quantitative in nature, and although this type of research has been of value, this field has relied too heavily on it (Rumsey & Harcourt, 2005; Thomson & Kent, 2001). In response to this criticism, there has been an increase in qualitative research into the issues surrounding facial disfigurement (e.g. Beaunie, Christopher & Keith, 2004; Wahl, Gjengedal & Hanestad, 2002). In recent years, the sheer complexities of the issues surrounding disfigurement have been recognised and the use of qualitative research in this area could be of value (Rumsey & Harcourt, 2005). Furthermore, because the processes and reasons behind views towards facial disfigurement are not fully understood, qualitative research will give a chance for theory and model building. Research into facial disfigurement has been criticised for being too empirical and lacking in theoretical understanding and direction; this is of no benefit to building interventions for this population (Kent, 2002). In addition, although many models and theories have been created, they often fail to encapsulate the complexity of societal attitudes (Rumsey & Harcourt, 2005). In addition, there has been a call for qualitative research for reasons behind public reactions (Gardiner et al., 2008).

For the reasons outlined above, this project has opted for qualitative research in order to explore the public views and perceptions of facial disfigurement. Behind this aim, is that in developing a greater understanding of the complex nature of public reactions to disfigurement, this may shed light or reasons behind the prejudice and stigmatisation reported in the literature. As recent research has suggested:

'research within the general population to establish the nature of their beliefs and attitudes towards disfigurement could be an essential step towards helping people with disfiguring conditions, as it may facilitate the development of community and clinical interventions for those distressed by the negative reactions of others' (Grandfield, Thomson, & Turpin, 2006; p. 823).

This may help to enhance the education of the public and in raising awareness surrounding facial disfigurement, and in turn reducing the prejudice and discrimination towards facial disfigurement. This will help improve the lives of those with a disfigurement, as public scrutiny is a vast contributor to their psychological problems.

Chapter 2
Methodology

2.1 Method rationale

Interpretative Phenomenological Analysis (referred to as IPA hereafter), was chosen as it allows direct access to participants inner worlds; it assumes a connection between what people say and their inner thoughts and feelings (Willag, 2008). It is concerned with making sense of the participants experience or account of a phenomenon. It acknowledges that any interpretation of data is bound to be influenced by the researcher: interpretation of the data is 'two-stage process' as the researcher is trying to make sense of the participant making sense of their inner world. This allows for the interpretation of the researcher to become part of the process (Smith, 2008) In addition, it is especially useful for exploring views and perceptions of a phenomena (Reid, Flowers, & Larkin, 2005). It also aims to produce an account of what and how the participants think about the phenomena, and finally aims to gain an insight into the participant's thoughts and beliefs that surround the topic under investigation.

This method is particularly of use to this research as this method allows interpretation of facial disfigurement from the participants point of view: this is needed to gain a stronger understanding of how the participants view and perceive facial disfigurement. Due to lack of understanding and theory, IPA allows for a unique interpretation of how the public view and experience facial disfigurement and it is especially designed to provide a theoretical groundwork for the topic under investigation (Brocki & Wearden, 2005).

Semi-structured interviews were used as they permit the researcher to directly observe the participants responses and feedback. In addition, it allows the participant to talk freely and direct the interview in terms of what is important for them (Smith, 2008). Semi-structured interviews are flexible in the fact that questions can be altered, or the order of them can be changed to suit the individual participant. In addition, they are convenient for the participant as they can be carried out in numerous locations and do not rely on a lab resource

2.2 Ethical considerations

Due to the sensitive nature of the topic, many ethical factors needed to be considered. Participants where told the nature of the research in detail. Before the interview commenced, the participants were given the chance to ask any questions or raise any concerns. They were reminded they did not have to answer any questions they were not uncomfortable with. The questions were kept open-ended and non-directive as this ensured that participants only spoke about what they were comfortable with, as they directed the conversation. In addition, no intrusive questions were asked. The confidentiality of the participants was kept; none of the participants are identifiable from the transcripts as their names were replaced with a participant number, and everyone was assured that no one would see their interview transcripts apart from the researcher. They were reminded that they could opt-out of the research at any time without question or consequence. In addition, informed consent was gained before any interviewing took place.

The posters used during the interviews were part of a poster campaign for the charity Changing Faces to raise public awareness. The posters where chosen as they were provided by a charity who had gained permission for the individual for these images to be shown to the public. It was thought that this would be more ethical than perhaps using images found on the internet.

2.3 Participants and recruitment

Three participants were recruited through Queen Margaret University, and three were recruited through word of mouth from the public. All participants where between the ages of eighteen and thirty and three males and three females were interviewed. The mean age was twenty six and this was a convenient sample. Three were students from the faculty of Media and Social Sciences and three were in full time employment. All participants were of British descent. For recruitment, an email was sent out via the university moderator to ask for volunteers; from this, three participants were recruited. Prior to this, no more volunteers came forward. The researcher therefore put out requests through word of mouth through and another three participants came forward. The participants were sent an information sheet to read and they then contacted the researcher if they wanted to take part.

2.4 Data collection

Semi-structured interviews were used as a method of data collection, as said to be appropriate for IPA (Willag, 2008). The interviews were recorded and transcribed. Seventeen thousand words of data was produced to be analysed. (For more details, see ethical approval).

2.5 Apparatus and Materials

A small digital recorder was used to record the interview and a set of pre-decided questions were used to guide the interview (see appendix 4). A computer was used to transcribe the interviews and an electronic recorder was used to record the interviews. A quiet room in Queen Margaret University or a quiet public place was used for the interviews. Three images were used, these posters pictured three individuals with different facial disfigurements. Three posters were used as stimulation for the participants, as it was thought that it might be a challenging topic to talk about. The first poster showed a woman with burns, the second a man with a genetic condition called neurofibromatosis, this results in excessive tissue growth, and the third a man with a tumour (see appendix 5- images 1-3.) In preparation for the interview, a pre- decided set of questions were created to guide the interview (see appendix 4). In addition, a consent form information sheet and debriefing sheet in line with QMU regulations were used.

2.6 Procedure

Once ethical approval had been granted from the university board, the participant recruitment (see above) for the interviews commenced. A time and place that was convenient for the participant was arranged for the interview. At the interview, they were given a chance to ask any questions, and if they were comfortable with being recorded, if they wished to take part the consent form was then signed. Once the participant was content, the interview commenced. At this point, the recorder was turned on. A definition was offered and a warm up question was asked (see question one of the interview set), to ease the participant into the interview. Although most of the questions in the interview schedule were used, the order changed from interview to interview and the participant widely dictated the interview. The questions were shaped to explore the participants views and perceptions of facial disfigurement, and furthermore to be opened-ended and non-directive.

The first part of the interview was always conducted first (see appendix 4). Subsequent to this, the posters were shown to the participants one at a time and the second set of questions were asked, this was to try to capture the essence of their perceptions of facial disfigurement. Some participants engaged more with the images than others did; some did not comment on them and others spent some time considering their content.

Socratic questioning was used and direct questioning was avoided; only probes were used, e.g. 'could you tell me a bit more about that?' The interviews lasted between 30 and 40 minutes and the debriefing and discussion a further 10 minutes. When the interview was finished, the participant was once again given the chance to ask any questions or raise any issues or concerns. In addition, they were asked how they found the experience of the interview, and if they had any suggestions for future interviews. After each interview, the researcher went to a quite space and wrote down any initial thoughts or ideas from the interview.

Once the six interviews were completed, they were transcribed by the researcher and analysed one by one using the steps of IPA, mapped out by Smith (2008). Each case was analysed individually, as IPA is an idiographic approach. Initially, the data was read, and reread, and from this initial thoughts, associations, contradictions, and questions that came to mind from reading the data were noted. Following this, the previous notes were used to label emerging themes with psychological meaning. After a list of themes had been drawn up for each case, all of the themes were examined to look for connections to create groups of themes; these groups were split into super-ordinate themes and sub-themes. This was done with each individual case, the analysis of the cases were then brought together to create a table of master themes, this was representative of the data as a whole. Some themes were left out, as the researcher felt they were not well represented by the text.

Chapter 3-Results

Through the principles of IPA, four major themes emerged across the data;

1. Those with a disfigurement were perceived to be different from normal.
2. The presence of a facial disfigurement was perceived to cause social awkwardness.
3. Having a facial disfigurement was conveyed to have negative effect on the lives of those with a disfigurement.
4. The participants spoke widely about facial disfigurement and society.

The super ordinate themes and their sub themes are mapped out below.

Super ordinate themes	Sub themes
Different from normal	Distinguished Separate
Social awkwardness	Adjustment to the disfigurement Perceived severity of the disfigurement Behaviour of the individual with the disfigureme
Perceived negative impact on life	Romance versus friendship Unattractiveness
Society and facial disfigurement	Belief of unfair treatment Negative depiction Emphasis on outward appearance Need for societal acceptance

Below is the researcher's interpretation of the themes presented above. Although the themes are presented as separate, the themes overlap and are interlinked with one another. These overlaps will be highlighted where appropriate.

3.1 Difference - distinction and separation

This theme is written as one integrated theme, as the sub themes were so heavily overlapped with one another. Many of the participants would often portray an image in their minds' of those with a facial disfigurement as being different to the rest of society; they were very distinguished in the participants minds due to their facial disfigurement:

> 'You would be able to pick them out like. They do stick out like a sore thumb...probably not the best way to put it. They are noticeable put it that way. I mean you see people with disfigurements and obviously you are going to notice them like, because they are different from everybody else' (Participant 1)

> 'It's something unusual about someone's face. I would say it is something about someone's face that makes them look different from normal.' (Participant 6)

The language used suggests that for them, being different is not positive - *'like a sore thumb'* and *'different from normal'*; this suggests a negative perception of them. This separates them in the participants mind from the rest of society. As expressed earlier, this difference appeared to separate individuals with disfigurement from the rest of society in the participants' minds. Only one participant was aware of this;

> 'I am aware of like, difference and how it sets you apart, puts you outside and again that whole sort of otherness. It sets people apart people from what society dictates as normal but I don't think there really should be a norm.' (Participant, 5)

Participant 5 expresses that for them, it is dangerous as it splits society; different versus normal. They experience it as a negative obsession, something dictated. This was the only participants who expressed being aware of this separation. This separation by the participants of 'us' and 'them' caused many participants to convey perceived difficulties in social interaction, with those with a facial disfigurement.

3.2 Super- ordinate theme- Social awkwardness

All of the participants expressed a perceived difficulty in social interaction with those with a facial disfigurement. This was expressed as a great concern of the participants. They conveyed that they believed many issues surrounding facial disfigurement would affect social interaction, including, the participants own adjustment to the facial disfigurement, the severity of the disfigurement, and how those with a facial disfigurement behaved during the social encounter.

3.2.1 Sub theme 1 - Adjustment to the facial disfigurement

Social interaction was conveyed to potentially improve when they had time to become adjusted to the facial disfigurement, as if they had not encountered a facial disfigurement before, this was seen to potentially cause shock or awkwardness:

> 'Maybe it's like the first five minutes, then it kinda goes away, the awkwardness I mean, well I mean it would still be there but you wouldn't notice it as much I don't think' (Participant 2).

Likewise;

> 'I think probably because it's not something you see every day. ...It might just take a bit if getting used to...it might be awkward in the first few seconds but as time went on, I think it would be ok. I might be a bit nervous about meeting them, but I don't think it would be as bad as I thought it would be.'(Participant 5)

It was a similar experience for these partakers; they all convey the potential shock or awkwardness of the first few seconds. However, prior to this, for them, there is great probability that this initial feeling will pass. This will cause it to be less evident in their minds, as it becomes less of a major concern. All the participants articulated this; it was very strongly conveyed. This sub-theme is interlinked with the first super ordinate theme; this sub-theme shows the potential for the perceived 'different from normal' to subside with adjustment. Furthermore, the second sub-theme is directly linked to the first as the perceived severity was said to affect adjustment to the facial disfigurement.

3.2.2 Sub-theme 2 - Perceived severity of the disfigurement

Perceived severity of the disfigurement was said by the participants to be a potential problem for successful social interaction because if it were a very severe facial disfigurement, from their point of view, this would take them longer to become used to. For example:

> 'When you are dealing with extreme example it might take a bit more than that. It just depends; I mean if they just had a lisp or a hair lip or something, I mean you would look over that pretty quickly. I mean this guy looks like he has a second jaw so that would take a while, you know what I mean like' (Participant 1)

The participants often related the perceived severity of the facial disfigurement to how long it would take them to adjust to the facial disfigurement. The more severe, the longer it would take them to feel at ease with it. As demonstrated in the following extract, many participants found it difficult to relate to the individual with a severe disfigurement, as they said they did not know how his disfigurement would have affected the individudal and how it could affect their potential meeting. The following participant contrasts the individual with a severe disfigurement to an individual with a less severe disfigurement (the individual in image 2 with the individual in image 3; appendix 5);

> 'I would find it easier being introduced to him, than to him. Because if you were introduced to this guy, you would except to be able to... well he looks like a normal bloke really, and you would expect him to have normal interests and be able to talk to him about normal things, like things you would be able to talk to anyone about. Whereas the other guy, you don't know what he would be able to do.' (Participant 6)

This participant is clearly expressing that from his point of view, the sheer severity of one man's disfigurement causes his apprehension to the social interaction, as he does not know how his disfigurement has affected him. However, with the other individual, as his face is more 'normal' to them, this perceived 'normalcy' is incredibly important, as the ability to have a normal conversation tames their nervousness. They appear unable to find familiar points of reference with the man with the severe disfigurement: this seems to disorientate them and make them concerned about their ability to interact with this individual.

As well as the perceived severity of the disfigurement, many of the participants said successful or unsuccessful social interaction could be determined by how the individual with the facial disfigurement behaved.

3.2.3 Sub-theme 3 - Behaviour of the individuals with the disfigurement

It was strongly represented that from the point of view of the participants, if the individual with the facial disfigurement appeared confident and self-assured that this would vastly improve the social encounter; as it would help them feel at ease with the facial disfigurement;

> 'I think if you knew that they were affected by it then that would make a difference to you, I mean if they were really affected by it then you probably will too, yeah. Whereas if they were like, to act as if it didn't exist then they would probably yeah, you might forget about it.' (Participant 1)

Similarly;

> 'I mean I would be surprised if she came up to me and was confident. Emmm, if she was confident and was chatting away to you, I don't think you would be that bothered' (Participant 6)

These extracts explain that the way the individual with the disfigurement is affected by their disfigurement is likely to affect how the participant reacted to them. If the individual with the disfigurement is affected by it, then it is likely the participant would be affected by it too. However, if the individual with the disfigurement was unaffected by it, in turn, the presence of a disfigurement was less likely to affect the participants to the same extent in the social interaction.

3.3 Perceived negative impact on life

All of the participants claimed facial disfigurement would have a profound negative impact on the life of the individual with the disfigurement. The participants identified key areas in which they thought that having a facial disfigurement might affect , including romantic relationships/friendships and attractiveness. Many participants expressed a great belief that those with a disfigurement would struggle profoundly in many areas of their lives. For example;

> 'I think they must have a dreadful time, everyone he walks past on the street is going to stare at him. It will probably make it difficult for them to have friends when they were a kid. Having a relationship would be almost

> *impossible.... That is the defining thing in their lives surely, I imagine it would be the major thing in his life.' (Participant 6)*

As demonstrated in the above extract, the majority of participants conveyed a great belief of a disfigurement causing the individual a great deal of distress and harmful impact in many areas of their lives. This major theme was present throughout all of the interviews without exception.

3.3.1 Sub-theme 1 - Romance versus friendship

The second sub-theme which emerged was that the participants viewed having a facial disfigurement, could result in the individuals having difficulties in romantic relationship and some of the participants expressed that they would not become romantically involved with a person with a facial disfigurement. This was in contrast to the participants stating that it would not affect their friendships. Firstly, the participants conveyed that those with a disfigurement may have trouble attracting partners;

> *'I guess people might have trouble attracting partners, I can't really think why...but that is what I think of. I guess because there is so much emphasis on good looks and people looking a certain way so...I guess if the first thing you notice about someone is their facial disfigurement, that might, that might create difficulties.' (Participant 3)*

Likewise;

> *'I mean, if you were in a club, I mean you wouldn't naturally go up to someone with a big scar across their face...Anyway, I mean it definitely wouldn't affect my friendship with **** but it might affect like whether I would go out with someone...it's like a physical aspect, like I wouldn't go out with someone who was obese. I mean you can't really help who you are attracted too.' (Participant 2)*

They describe the facial disfigurement as like a barrier; that with a disfigurement you cannot talk to others in order to initiate a romantic relationship. The facial disfigurement will cause social difficulties; participant 3 makes sense of this through society's emphasis on good looks. Participant 2 contrasts the effect of having a facial disfigurement if you were approach someone for romance, with its affect on friendship. Whilst it would not affect this participants friendship, it would affect them approaching someone in a club. Participant 2 makes sense of this through stating that one cannot control whom one is attracted to, suggesting they assume they would not be attracted to someone with a facial disfigurement. Likewise, another participant conveyed facial disfigurement would not affect friendships;

> 'I mean if you were friends with someone it obviously wouldn't make a difference. I mean I can't speak for the whole population but certainly with me, looks don't matter in a friendship! Even in a relationship, like a romantic one or whatever, I would hope it wouldn't make a difference to me but I guess it could affect if you were attracted to someone, if it was really extreme maybe.' (Participant 5)

The participant is expressing that a disfigurement, from their point of view, would never affect a friendship. They express an inner struggle by admitting that it may affect them being attracted to someone but they also expresses a wish that it would not affect them in this way. This sub-theme was expressed by four of the participants

3.3.3 Sub-theme 3 - Unattractiveness

Closely tied to sub-theme 2, in sub-theme 3 it emerged that those with a facial disfigurement were perceived to be unattractive, which was one of the perceived causes of difficulties in attracting partners:

> 'But if I was out for a night out and I seen her, and I saw a beautiful looking girl, you wouldn't go chatting her up, you would surely chat up the beautiful looking girl.' (Participant 1)

Participant 1 separates those with a disfigurement and those who are attractive, ultimately suggesting that those with a disfigurement are not attractive. It was expressed that facial disfigurement could stop the participants approaching someone for romantic purposes. It was strongly conveyed that acquiring a facial disfigurement would result in the loss of attractiveness. This is linked with the previous sub-themes as the participants further spoke of the disfigurement affecting the individuals' appearance. The following example portrays the views of many of the participants, but it should be noted not all participants portrayed this view:

> 'That's the thing, if you go from being a pretty girl sitting in a pub, and somehow a glass comes flying in your face and then you are disfigured, like to go to that, from being like a really gorgeous girl to being disfigured would be really hard. Maybe if you were good looking before then it is almost harder for you because you have lost more.'(Participant 2)

It is explained here that there is a belief that being disfigured, would result in one losing their looks. Participant 2 contrasts being 'gorgeous' with being 'disfigured'. To them this would be a great loss and it would have a negative effect on the individual's life. Another participant further conveyed the perceived unattractiveness of those with a disfigurement:

> 'I mean fair enough when you are starting at the other end of the scale (the beauty scale), but she might have a brilliant personality and be helpful and that type of thing.' (Participant 1)

For this participant, those with a disfigurement are 'at the other end of the beauty scale', suggesting that that are not only unattractive, but they are at the opposite end of the scale; a strong statement. Participant 1 associates facial disfigurement with being highly unattractive, this association appears to be strong from the participant's point of view. However, the participant does suggest that their personality might make a difference in how they perceive them.

3.4 Super -ordinate theme 4 - Facial disfigurement and society

One theme present throughout all of the interviews was the participants speaking of facial disfigurement and its place within our society. All of the participants conveyed a significant belief that those with a disfigurement would suffer from prejudice and stigmatization at the hands of society. They also spoke of how facial disfigurement was negatively portrayed by our society and our cultural values. All of the participants also described that they felt society had a role to play in decreasing prejudice and discrimination towards those with a facial disfigurement. There appeared to be great awareness of how those with a facial disfigurement are negatively treated; this was often the essence of the interview.

3.4.1 Sub- theme 1 - Unjust treatment

The first sub-theme to emerge was the belief of the unjust treatment ,of those with a facial disfigurement ,by society. Many expressed this belief from personal experience. For example, one participant spoke of the effect of public reactions on his friend, who acquired a facial disfigurement from the result of a traumatic car accident:

> 'Just on top of the accident and then having to deal with all the other shit on top of that. I mean it's not fair that he has to deal with everyone else's reactions on top of all the other shit. It's like a viscous circle; it makes things more difficult for him.'(Participant 2)

This participant conveyed that their friend has been poorly treated by society, they describe how this increases their friend's difficulties. From this participants point of view it distresses them, as they perceive it as being unjust to their friend. Furthermore, it was articulated that many participants felt society might make a conscious effort to avoid those with a disfigurement. The following example was typical:

> Eh, I mean I wouldn't have a problem with it but I mean some people would maybe think like...that they would try and avoid them at all costs, I don't know why but...that's just what some people are like, but I don't have a problem with it.' (Participant 1)

This was common for the participants; many conveyed a belief that society would avoid them or treat them in a negative manner. However, interestingly none of them articulated that they would personally treat them in this way. All of the participants expressed that they thought this treatment and avoidance was unjust. This first sub-theme is highly interlinked was the second sub-theme in that they again believed society was being unjust to those with a facial disfigurement.

3.4.2. Sub-theme 2 – Negatively depicted by society

The second related sub-theme to emerge was a belief of the participants that facial disfigurement was portrayed as a very negative phenomenon in society. One area commonly spoke about was how facial disfigurement is depicted by the media. The following example is typical;

> 'Maybe if TV didn't depict them like this it would be different, because they are depicted as so different to the rest of us, it is like 'us' and 'them'. Almost like, they are a different species or something, no that is a bit extreme, but our society is very cruel if you are a bit different. It makes you think that someone with a disfigurement is going to suffer at the hands of society, it's a shame. Even when you think of the word 'disfigure', it's not a nice word, a bit like 'deformity', it doesn't have nice connotations.' (Participant 5)

This negative depiction was said to lead the participants to believe that those with a disfigurement will be treated negatively too, further linking this sub theme to the previous. It was conveyed that those with a disfigurement are depicted as separate from the rest of society, participant 5 describes the negative language that society uses to describe them, this was articulated in many of the interviews. One participant spoke of how different areas of society may perceive disfigurement in a different way:

> 'But I think if you are a bit more in a sub-culture...you know Goth or whatever you might be a bit more accepting of someone who is different. Eeemmm, certainly from my personal experience the sub-cultures tend to view these things differently.' (Participant 4).

Participant 4 describes how a culture they are part of views disfigurement differently. They speak of sub cultures, and their acceptance of those who are different. From their point of view, sub-cultures have a different meaning of beauty and in their view certain areas of society are more accepting,

3.4.3 Sub-theme 3 - emphasis on outward appearance

Closely related to how those with a disfigurement are depicted by society, it was suggested that society's negative depiction and treatment of them might be due to cultures obsession with outward appearances:

> ' I guess because there is so much emphasis on good looks and people looking a certain way so...I guess if the first thing you notice about someone is their facial disfigurement, that might, that might create difficulties.' (Participant 3)

Similarly:

> 'But I mean a large part of society's beauty ideal is having perfect skin...so it like when I see I all these adverts...I feel...well I don't really feel good enough' (Participant 4)

Society's emphasis on good looks has caused this participant to have a negative perception of themselves, this has resulted in them perceiving society's obsession with appearance as a negative factor. Furthermore, another participant articulated the harmful effect of this obsession on those with a facial disfigurement:

> 'it just shows how much value people place on looks and it seems they almost see themselves as better if they are considered better looking than someone else. I think society has to stop placing so much emphasis on looks before people will stop ridiculing the likes of those with a facial disfigurement.' (Participant 5)

From this participant's point of view, society's obsession with looks may cause individuals to perceive themselves as better than those with a facial disfigurement, as society depicts them as having a superior appearance. They believe the way to stop this is for society to decrease its high importance on the values of good looks. This was a common thought of the participants; they believed society had a huge part to play in preventing prejudice towards those with a facial disfigurement.

3.3.4 Sub-theme 4 - Call for social acceptance

It was widely expressed in the interviews that society had a role in decreasing their negative treatment and the way in which we as a society depict these individuals:

> 'I mean it's a thing society wants to change really because...like...emmm I mean if your good looking, you'll get away with an awful lot more shit like. You would though. I have seen fellows getting away with stuff; I mean you wouldn't think butter would melt in their mouths.' (Participant 1)

Likewise:

> 'I guess I would say that society should learn to be more accepting and be a bit more sensitive to their feelings..., maybe people just don't think. I think they need to be more aware. But then again some people are just selfish and horrible, but I think a lot of it is ignorance and people just not thinking.'(Participant 5)

Both of these extracts convey all of the participants' belief that society should change the negative treatment of those with a facial disfigurement. It was expressed that society needs to change it perceptions of facial disfigurement; as one participant explains how they are depicted in many areas of society:

> 'Yeh all kinds of art from painting, films, photography. Its kinda like what is on the outside reflects what is in the inside, which is a very old fashioned way of thinking. I mean as an artist I understand the strong metaphorical potential of it and if it affects people's lives, then I think we, we definitely think we need to re- think it... I think there needs to be a huge change.' (Participant 4)

In this extract, participant 4 articulates how they feel disfigurement and difference is depicted throughout society. They speak of 'what is on the outside reflects what is in the outside'. Although they can understand the strong impact of this metaphor, they do not think it should be at the price of upsetting people, therefore, they believe society needs to change. This theme has shown that there was great awareness of societal attitudes towards those with a disfigurement. In addition, there was a vast belief that society should change their beliefs and behaviours towards these individuals.

5.5 Summary of results

The first three super-ordinate themes and their sub-themes all share an overall similarity; they all portray a negative image of those with a disfigurement, and of their lives. Although theme 4 shares this negative view, in that those with a facial disfigurement were believed to be poorly treated and depicted by society; this theme also revealed a great awareness of how unjust this treatment and depiction of those with a facial disfigurement is. This shows a positive side to public views and perceptions of facial disfigurement.

Chapter 5 Discussion

This section will discuss the findings with reference to previous research; it will be compared and contrasted. Implications and future directions for further research will be highlighted. Possible limitations of this research will also be stated.

5.1 Theme one- Different from normal- distinction/separation

The finding that they are perceived as distinguished from others is not unexpected ;research has found that those with a disfigurement capture the attention of participants (Ackerman et al., 2009). This visibility often separated individuals with a disfigurement in the participants mind from the rest of society; often using language such as 'us' and 'them' and categorising them. The social model of disability highlights the concept of 'otherness' in the stigmatisation process (Taleporos and Mcabe, 2002: Smith ,2007). This is in line with the results, as the participants did not view them as normal, they instead categorised those with a disfigurement as 'other', and apart from the rest of society. This is what Goffman (1963) refers to as social stigmatisation. Furthermore, they may 'stick out' in the participants mind, as humans tend to perceive negative features ahead of positive features, that may fade into the background, i.e. the facial disfigurement will stand out, as it is considered a negative attribute (Raskin, 2009). This would hold true on the phenomena of facial disfigurement and in line with the findings of this research.

It has been suggested that we categorise individuals as 'normal' and 'abnormal' as live in a society that views everyone is relation to a 'norm' of a phenomena, e.g. we are compared to a 'normal' height and weight. Turning to the disability literature, Davis (2006) points out that the word 'normal' only entered our language in 1840. As a result of this, it is how our society that has created the concept of normality that has caused us to categorise people as 'normal' and 'abnormal'. If one turns to the participants construction as those with a disfigurement as 'not normal', this may be due to society's construction of normality, which has caused us to view normality as the ideal, and in turn view variation from this norm as something which 'must be minimised'(Davis, 2006;p.6). He concludes by suggesting that our society need a new way of constructing normality, so we can view it in a different and more positive light. If society can find a new way of viewing the 'abnormal', those with a facial disfigurement may not be viewed in such a different and negative way.

Allport (1954) established that we categorise individuals into differing categories to simplify our chaotic social world and in order reduce our cognitive load. Furthermore, the classification of those with a disfigurement as different, may be part of the reason for the reported discrimination and prejudice:

'How we classify ourselves and others along these multiple social criteria has a significant impact on intergroup relations... categorisation has played a central role in explorations of person perception. It is now understood to be an integral part of the explanation for prejudice and discrimination' (Crisp, 2002; p.416).

Due to this finding, as our categorisation of those with a disfigurement, to an extent causes prejudice. If society were to find new ways of viewing those with a disfigurement, as a valued and normal part of society, this may aid in reducing discrimination. This has been conveyed in the disability literature:

'Changes in the construction of disability require a fundamental cognitive shift away from the stereotypical view that the young white able-bodied male is king, and towards the valuing of all individuals for the contribution that they make to the richness of the world in which we all live' (Frankish, 2002; p.416).

This calls for a change in society's conception surrounding facial disfigurement, in recognising they can contribute to society in the same way as everybody else. If society can see their ability, this may go some way to changing society's categorisation of these individuals as differing from normality.

5.2 Theme 2- Social Awkwardness

This theme is particularly of interest, as every participant expressed social interaction as an area of concern or difficulty. This finding has shed light on why society may avoid or act apprehensively around those with a disfigurement. This finding can be explained in relation to the literature. It has been found that the presence of a person with a facial disfigurement can cause negative perceptions of how well they can socially function (Marlene, 2005). Part of this preoccupation with social interaction may be due to the finding that it causes great unease in individuals

(Jones and Stone, 1995). This unease may cause them to become overly concerned when encountering those with a disfigurement. Many participants appeared apprehensive, due to the belief that the facial disfigurement may affect communication. This is in line with previous research findings that the location of the disfigurement, in terms of how it may affect communication, can influence their response (Gardiner, 2008).

5.2.1 Sub-theme 1- Perceived severity of the disfigurement

As regards to severity of the disfigurement, this has been found to affect social interaction in other research (Rumsey & Harcourt, 2005; Yamin et al., 2004). As outlined here, *'Visibility and obtrusiveness of a stigma are important mediators of the interaction between the stigmatised and the 'normal world'* (Taleporos and McCabe, 2002; p.972). This suggests that how visible the disfigurement is, is important for social interaction; it acts like a barrier to the 'normal' world. This suggests that in order to improve social relations, society needs to break down this 'barrier'.

5.2.2 Sub-theme 2- Adjustment to the facial disfigurement

With regards to the finding that participants conveyed the belief that after the initial encounter with those with a facial disfigurement, they could become adjusted to it: to the researchers knowledge, this is not discussed to any great extent in the literature. This finding points to the possible influence of society being familiar with facial disfigurement. In addition, it has been found that we have 'neophobia' (Kremer & Schermbrucker, 2006), i.e. we have an aversion to the new and different. This may result in individuals being uncomfortable around facial disfigurement, if they have not encountered anything like it before. This result highlights the importance of educating society at all levels; school and work environments, to raise awareness of the issues surrounding facial disfigurement, so to prepare the public for encountering facial disfigurement. The charity Changing Faces has made a valuable start to this process; in aiming to educate the public and raise awareness. The findings of this research further conveys the importance of this charity's work.

5.2.3 Sub-theme 3- Behaviour of the individual with the disfigurement

Many participants articulated that if the individual with the disfigurement was confident and self-assured, this would improve the social interaction for them; due to it making the participants feel more at ease. However if individual with the disfigurement was uncomfortable and nervous, this would in turn make them anxious in the social encounter.

Alan Partridge has widely conveyed his beliefs that people are apprehensive coming into social interaction, due to fear of not knowing how to act around those with a facial disfigurement. In addition, he has emphasised the role of those with a disfigurement in successful interaction. As discussed in the literature review, findings have supported the role of the individual with the disfigurement making a significant difference to social interaction. This finding confirms the public's belief in this strategy as being successful, in helping them feel at ease with the presence of a facial disfigurement. However, due to the finding that those with a disfigurement can often suffer from psychological and social problems, often due to public ridicule, it is argued here that the role of society changing their prejudices, and behaviour towards disfigurement, must play a role in the successful social interaction. It is thought that a large part of successful adjustment lies in successful interaction with other members of the public (Ong et al., 2007). This accentuates the importance of society adjusting to those with disfigurements, to help these individuals self-regulate with their disfigurement.

5.3 Theme three- perceived negative impact on life.

All of the participants perceived facial disfigurement as having a potential negative impact on the individual's life. This is line with the research. Partridge (1990) stated that one of the myths surrounding disfigurement was that society held the belief that those with a disfigurement could not lead a successful or happy life. This research confirms that this myth is still strongly held in our culture. This research extends on previous research by providing details of how this myth is held and in what areas of life.

These results are also in line with the ITA carried out by Changing Faces, as 90% of individuals viewed them to have a lower quality of life. This study demonstrates the sheer prevalence of these beliefs. This ITA is also in line with the finding of perceived difficulties in career, as the ITA found the belief that they would have lower success in life. Furthermore, many of the participants perceived them to be unattractive, which is also in line with the finding of the ITA and a further study which found those with a facial disfigurement were perceived to be unattractive(Marlene, 2005),. As our society often couples attractiveness with 'goodness' (Stevenage & Mckay, 1999), this is in turn, this is likely to cause people to associate perceived 'unattractiveness' with negative attributes. Those with a disfigurement were perceived as unattractive, and in turn, poses negative attributes.

Sub-theme 1 and 2- Romance versus friendship and Unattractiveness

These two sub-themes will be discussed together as they highly overlap. The main reason given by the participants for a facial disfigurement causing problems in romantic relationship was that they perceived them to be unattractive. It appears likely that a facial disfigurement would not affect a friendship ,as a friendship does not require the participant to take into account the individuals appearance, and in turn the facial disfigurement. These results are dissimilar to previous research in that it has been reported that having a facial disfigurement will result in them having difficulty building friendship (research), however this research reveals that some may not see it as a problem when it comes to friendship. In addition, the way in which facial disfigurement may affect romantic relationships is not discussed to any great deal in the literature to the researchers knowledge.

The finding that they were perceived as unattractive, and that previous looks will be lost because of acquiring a disfigurement, may be understood in relation to the evolutionary literature. Firstly, the face is particularly important in judgements of beauty (Furnham, Lavancy, & McClelland, 2001). Evolutionary theory would state that we have evolved underlying psychological mechanisms, (e.g. facial symmetry) towards certain cues of attractiveness that advertise gene quality (Gangestad & Thornhill, 1997; 1999). Furthermore symmetrical faces are perceived as more attractive (Cardenas & Harris, 2006;Rhodes et al., 1998; 1999;). As a facial disfigurement inevitably will result in asymmetry, this may cause people to perceive them as unattractive. However, this research does not take individual differences or other factors of attractiveness into account; in addition, it is thought to lack ecological validity (Swiami & Furnham, 2008).

The finding that symmetric faces are considered more attractive has been refuted; individual taste has been demonstrated to be as important as universal taste in perceptions of facial attractiveness. (Honekopp, 2006). The reasons behind facial disfigurement being viewed as unattractive are likely to be more complex than the evolutionary research suggests, e.g. it has been suggested that in evolutionary models: *'cultural complexity and behavioural diversity are sidelined, becoming irrelevant as the 'universal' elements of human development are revealed'* (Jackson & Rees, 2007, p922). This statement is relevant to facial disfigurement, as it has been shown that it is to a certain extent a culturally defined phenomenon (Elkes, 1990;Partridge, 1990;Sullivan, 2001). Therefore, an evolutionary approach will not be sufficient to explain the complex issues surrounding disfigurement. It has been highlighted by researchers that the evolutionary approach widely ignores the social agenda, and that there needs to be a link in research in the social and biological domains, and with evolutionary research, the biological is always prevailing (Shakespeare and Erickson, 2000). It is clear from these results that there is a social factors in society's view of those with a disfigurement.

The perceived unattractiveness of those with a facial disfigurement could cause a wider view of the disfigurement having a negative effect on their lives, due to the effect of the physical attractiveness stereotype (Dion, Berschfield and Walster ,1972). It has been claimed that individuals that are more 'attractive' are perceived by society to be more successful in life and have better personalities (Eagley et al., 1991). In addition, advertising and magazines bombard society with models with flawless skin and faces; our society has come to take this as a beauty ideal. This is in turn likely to cause us to perceive something like facial disfigurement, which is very different from this beauty ideal, as not attractive. Partridge (1990) has warned of the danger on such advertising, as this may increase prejudice towards those with a facial disfigurement. From this research, it would suggest that many individuals do perceive these individuals as very unattractive. The above discussion is also relevant to theme 4- sub-theme 3.

With no exceptions, the participants predominately viewed facial disfigurement as something that would have a profound effect in many areas of their lives. This may account for pity and prejudice towards those with a facial disfigurement. The myths surrounding disfigurement have no basis (Coutinho, 2006), as people with disfigurements can lead normal and thriving lives (Changing Faces, 2008). Changing Faces (2008), have highlighted that society perceive that only attractive people can lead successful lives; this research has found that this myth is still present in society. This finding supports the need for society to change and for there to be more education and awareness building to help diminish this negative perception of those with a facial disfigurement, as this negative perception will no doubt contribute further to the social difficulties experienced by those with a facial disfigurement.

5.4 Theme four- facial disfigurement and society

All of the participants spoke a great deal of how they felt those with a disfigurement are treated and depicted by our society; this was profoundly negative in nature.

5.4.1 Sub-theme 1= negative treatment

The reality of this belief is well documented in the literature, as discussed in the literature review. (E.g. Changing Faces, 2008;Macgregor ,1990; Rumsey & Bull, 1996). What should be emphasized here is the significant awareness of the participants of how these individuals are treated. This could be used in contrast to the ITA carried out by Changing Faces (2008) that claimed the public are often unaware of their prejudices. Furthermore, they all appeared to be aware that this treatment was unjust, and conveyed a strong belief that society should change.

In addition, participant 4 used the example of sub-cultures; that the 'Goth' culture is more accepting of facial disfigurement and difference . This implies it is avoidable that our society perceives disfigurement as a negative entity; we can view difference in a positive light. Furthermore, research could look at ways in which different areas of society may observe facial disfigurement in an optimistic way; this could encourage other areas of society to consider disfigurement in a different manner. It should be noted that this theme is highly related to theme one, as our separation of them as different can lead to prejudice and stigmatisation (Allport, 1954; Goffman, 1963).

5.4.2 Sub-theme 4- Negative depiction

The finding that participants conveyed that they felt facial disfigurement was depicted very negatively within out society is interesting. Although the truth of this negative depiction is well documented (Rouche, 2008: Wardle & Boyce, 2009), the finding that the participants showed great awareness of this suggests that it has not gone unnoticed by the public.

Very recent research has found that those with a facial disfigurement are extremely under-represented in the media, and when they are, they are portrayed in a negative way, and they often do not have a major role to play. In addition, stereotypes and myths of facial disfigurement are often enhanced. This research has advised that those with a disfigurement be given a more positive role in the media, this may help challenge societal prejudices and stigmatisation. Furthermore, it advised that in order to change the negative depictions of facial disfigurement in the media, individuals which a disfigurement must be made a valued part of the work force. Interventions could follow one similar to ones aimed at recruiting more disabled people to work within the media (Wardle & Boyce, 2009).

The finding that we are more likely to remember information that is unswerving from our present categorisation (Rothbart *et al.*, 1979), is likely to result in individuals perception of those with a facial disfigurement as being confirmed, as they will only acknowledge information that fits with their present view. Therefore, if society continues to depict these individuals in a negative way, and people internalise these categorisations, they are likely to prevail. This suggests that if we change the negative depiction, this in turn may result in perceptions and views of disfigurement changing.

5.4.3 Sub-theme 3- Emphasis on outward appearance

The effect of our society's emphasis on outward appearance is discussed in literature review (e.g. Dion, Berschfield and Walster, 1972), and above in theme three.

5.4.4 .Sub-theme 4- Need for societal acceptance

The disability literature highlights the role of society changing it attitudes towards the stigmatised group (Davis, 2005;Thomson & Kent, 2001). The results of this research point towards society sharing this view, and although the results cannot be generalised, every participant expressed this belief. Further quantitative research would need to carried out in order to confirm this finding.

One reason for the view for to society change was due to their personal encounters of how the negative treatment of society treated those with a disfigurement. The literature has documented the effect of discrimination on these individuals (Lansdown et al., 1997; Moss & Rosser, 2008; Rumsey & Harcourt, 2003, 2005). The participants appeared very aware of the effect of social ridicule. This awareness, in addition to their belief that society should change, suggests that some members of society would be willing to attempt to reconsider their prejudice , and treat those with a disfigurement with more consideration. However, these results suggest that individuals may need a 'push' to change their negative perceptions. Although there was a great awareness of society treating and depicting these individuals inadequately, and a recognised need for change, they seemed unaware of their own negative perceptions and beliefs surrounding facial disfigurement.

5.5 Conclusion

This project has aimed to explore public views and perceptions of facial disfigurement, this aim was achieved through using IPA analysis. The results of this investigation uncover a predominately negative perception of facial disfigurement; as discussed throughout. Overall, participants had profound difficulty with connecting facial disfigurement to a happy and successful life. This is in line with previous research as discussed above However, this research has uncovered that there was great awareness of the participants surrounding the negative treatment and depiction of those with a disfigurement. In addition, they all articulated that society needed to change this.

This is beginning to be done. Charities like Changing Faces are battling to change the negative views and depiction of those with a facial disfigurement. Due to the extent of this problem, society will need to work hard to turn this around.

One way in which this could be achieved is prejudice and stigmatisation reduction techniques. A recent review of the prejudice reduction literature has concluded psychologists still have a large amount of work to do before we have an understanding of how best to diminish prejudice. The research literature 'does not reveal whether, when, and why interventions reduce prejudice in the world' (Paluck & Green, 2009;p.360). This is due to lack of validity in the existing research, and there is a need more field research to demonstrate the usefulness of interventions to reduce prejudice(Paluck & Green, 2009). The stigmatisation reduction strategies also suffer from similar problems, and there also need more research to confirm their effectiveness (Heljnders & Van Der Meij, 2006).

Along with this, society can try to find different ways about thinking about facial disfigurement. The social model of disability:

'challenges the traditional view of disability as a medical tragedy, and replaces it with a view of disability as a social oppression...arguing that disability is socially constructed not biologically determined.' (Shakespeare, Gillespie-Sells, & Davis, 1996; p.3.)

This suggests that if facial disfigurement is socially constructed, we can begin to attempt to socially construct it in a different manner. If we recognise how we define it as a culture, we can begin to turn this around.

On a more positive note, there was great awareness of societal prejudice and the participants expressed a great belief that society should change. Society acknowledging their behaviours, and depiction of those with a facial disfigurement may be the first step in society changing. Every participant expressed a belief in society's responsibility to change; this shows that there may be willingness from other members of society. In order for this change to come about, society must learn to be more accepting of difference and may need to find a new way of thinking about facial disfigurement;

'Hopefully it can instil a positive motivation for genuinely embracing difference and, in turn, not only understanding but also dealing with conflict... It requires the simple recognition that, psychologically, it is difference that continues to makes life interesting, challenging and enjoyable – and that can make all the difference.' (Kremer & Schermbrucker, 2006;p.163)

This quote suggests that we should celebrating diversity, instead of perceiving it as something negative. Those with a facial disfigurement have much to offer in demonstrating that they can contribute to society, e.g. in a work environment, in the same way any 'normal' individual can. What is stopping them is society rejecting them as normal human beings. The media and public services have a responsibility in changing the views of difference and facial disfigurement (Wardle & Boyce, 2009). Our culture needs to find ways of embracing difference and seeing past the disfigurement, to the human qualities underneath. After all;

'there is a great deal of pain and suffering involved in being defined as 'facially disfigured', but why should society inflict such punishment on persons who have done no wrong and based on such arbitrary criteria and spurious beliefs?" (Elks,1990; p.5).

5.6 Limitations of research

This research cannot be generalised to the population as a whole. However, the aim of this study was not to generalise but to view in depth the views and perceptions of facial disfigurement. IPA instead aims to gain a rich, personal account of the phenomenon under investigation. Although the results cannot be generalised, they can indicate areas of interest for further research and theory and model building.

One possible limitation is that the topic of the research may have attracted individuals who had a great deal to say on the topic or a had a particular interest at the topic at hand. For example, three of the participants had personal experiences with facial disfigurement. Namely, two of them had friends who had acquired facial disfigurements through car accidents and one of the participants had a partner who had suffered from Bell's Palsy. This could arguably affect their view or perceptions of facial disfigurement, as they have had a personal experience of it.

It could be argued that due to the taboo nature of the topic, the participants would say what they felt was socially desirable, e.g. none of the participants explicitly stated that they had a negative view of those with a facial disfigurement: they referred to the rest of society as having this negative view. Due to social interest, it is unlikely participants would not have explicitly said they had an overt prejudice.

5.7 Future directions

One potential area for further research is cross-cultural, to see if other cultures view disfigurement in a similar way to western cultures. This may help select out the cultural and biological aspects of views and perceptions of disfigurement.

This project looked at facial disfigurement as a general topic. It may be beneficial to psychological understanding to look at how views differ towards differing kinds of disfigurement, e.g. acquired and congenital, as the aetiology of the disfigurement may affect public perceptions.

5.7 Personal contribution

This section was considered relevant for this research as IPA acknowledges the role of the researcher in the process. Therefore, the researcher personal view and motivations behind the research are highly relevant. This section will be written in the first person.

I was drawn to this topic for many reasons. The reason I chose this particular angle, is that after reading the literature and research, it became apparent that there was a huge lack of understanding surrounding the public reactions to facial disfigurement. One particular reason I was drawn to it, was due to a personal experience when I was younger, I experienced public reactions to facial disfigurement first hand, and this has resulted in me having a great interest in the topic. I believe the reasons behind public reactions are more complex, which one theory, e.g. evolutionary, cannot explain. There is something about facial disfigurement, which makes people very uneasy. Having experienced public reactions first hand, I believe researching public views and perceptions in more depth will help reduce public discrimination and prejudice towards those with a facial disfigurement.

Although many may believe my personal experience may cause me to have a subjective effect on collecting and data analysis , I was highly carful and aware not to let my personal feelings and experiences affect my interviews and data analysis. I achieved this through taking a very profession stance in the interviews, in the sense that it was not a personal conversation were my views became apparent, and making sure that I only asked open-ended questions to ensure what the participant said was not affected by anything that I said. In addition, my personal experience was in the past, and it does not affect me largely. I found the experience of this undertaking and completing this research, above all, interesting, and I extremely enjoyed it.

References

Ackerman, J.M., Becker, D.V., Mortensen, C.R., Sasaki, T., Neuberg, S.L. and Kenrick, D.T. (2009). A pox on the mind: Disjunction of attention and memory in the processing of physical disfigurement. *Journal of Experimental Social Psychology, 4, 1-8.*

Allport, G.W. (1954). The nature of prejudice. *Reading, MA: Addison–Wesley.*

Baker, C. (1992). Factors associated with rehabilitation in head and neck cancer. *Cancer Nursing, 15, 395-400.*

Baumeister, R., and Leary, M.R. (1995). The need to belong: desire for interpersonal attachments as a fundamental human motivation. *Psychological Bulletin, 117, 497-529.*

Bessell, A., Moss, T. M. (2007). Evaluating the effectiveness of psychology interventions for individuals with visible differences: A systematic review of the empirical literature. *Body image 4, 227-238.*

Brockia, J.M., and A.J. Wearden. (2005). A critical evaluation of the use of interpretative phenomenological analysis (IPA) in health psychology. *Psychology & Health,21,1,87— 108*

Bull, R. (1979). The psychological significance of facial deformity, *in M. Cook and G. Wilson (eds) Love and attraction. Oxford:Pergamon.*

Burriss, R.P., Rowland, H.M., and Little, A.C.(2009).Facial Scaring enhances men's attractiveness for short-term relationships. *Personality and individual differences, 46, 213-217.*

Cash, T. F. (1990). The psychology of physical appearance: Aesthetics, attributes, and images. *In T. F. Cash & T. Pruzinsky (Eds.), Body images: Development, deviance, and change (pp.51–79). New York: Guilford Press.*

Changing Faces (2006). Changing Faces on Face Transplantation. Face Transplantation. 1-4.

Changing faces. (2007). Prevalence rates of disfigurement within the population. *(unpublished)*

Changing Faces .(2008).The face equality campaign- the evidence, *Public attitudes survey. Unpublished.*

Clarke, A. (1999). Psychosocial aspects of facial disfigurement, problems, management and the role of a lay-led organization. *Psychology, Health and Medicine, 4, 127–142.*

Clarke, A., Rumsey, N., Collin, JOR, and Wyn-Williams, M .(2003).Psychological distress associated with disfiguring eye conditions. *Eye, 17, 35-40.*

Countinho, W. (2006). 'Don't let the way I look affect the way you see me'. *Changing Faces: London.*

Crisp, R.J.(2002).Social categorisation: Blurring the boundaries. *The psychologist, Vol.15, No.12, 612-615.*

Davis, L.J. (2006). Constructing normalcy: The Bell Curve, the Novel, and the Intervention of the Disabled Body in the Nineteenth Century, P3-15. *In the Disability Studies Reader, Second Edition.*

Dion K, Berscheid., E,Walster E. 1972. What is beautiful is good. *J. Personal. Soc. Psychol.* 24:285–90

Eagly, A.H., Ashmore, R.D., Makhijani, M.G. and Longo, L.C.(1991). What is beautiful is good but...: a meta analytic review of the research on the physical attractiveness stereotype. *Psychological Bulletin, 110, 109-28.*

Elks, M. A. (1990). Another look at facial disfigurement. *Journal of rehabilitation, Vol. 36, 56- 63.*

Fauerbach, J.A. (2008). From survival to socialisation: A longitudinal study of body image in survivors of severe burn injury. *Journal of Psychosomatic Research, 64, 205-221.*

Frankish, P. (2005). Disability. *The psychologist, Vol.18, No. 7, 416-417.*

Furness, P., Garrud, P., Faulder, A, & Swift, J. (2006). Coming to terms: A Grounded Theory of Adaption to Facial Surgery in Adulthood. *Journal of health psychology, 11, 453-465.*

Gardiner, M.D., Topps, A., Richardson, G., Sacker, A., Clarke, A., and Butler, P.E.M. (2008). Differential judgements about disfigurement: the role of location, age and gender in decisions made by observers. *Journal of Plastic, Reconstructive and Aesthetic Surgery, 1-5.*

Goffman, E. (1963). *Stigma: Notes on the management of spoiled identity.* New Jersey: Prentice-Hall.

Grandfield, T.A., Thomson, A.R., and Turpin, G. (2005). An attitudinal study of responses to a range of dermatological conditions using implicit attitude test. *Journal of health psychology, vol 10, no 6, 812-829.*

Greenhouse, S.(2003). Lifetime affliction leads to US bias suit. *The New York Times(p. A08. March 30).*

Harcourt, D., Rumsey, N. (2008).Psychology and visible difference. *The Psychologist, Vol. 21, No. 6, 486-489.*

Heason, S., & Kent, G. (2003). Vitiligo: More than a skin disease. (www.shef.ac.uk/socst/Shop/Heason)

Heljnders, M., and Van Der Meij, S.(2006). The fight against stigma: An overview of stigma-reduction strategies and interventions. Psychology, Health & Medicine, 11,3, 353 – 363

Hodson, G. and Costello, K. (2007). Interpersonal disgust, Ideological Orientations, and Dehumanisation as Predictors of Intergroup Attitudes. *Psychological Science, 18, 8, 691-698.*

Honekopp, J. (2006). Once more: Is beauty in the eye of the beholder? Relative contributions of private and shared taste to judgments of facial attractiveness. *Journal of experimental psychology, Vol. 32, No.2, 199-209.*

Houston, V., and Bull, R. (1994). Do people avoid sitting next to someone who is facially disfigured? *European Journal of Social Psychology, 24, 279-284.*

Jackson, S. and Rees, A. (2007) 'The Appalling Appeal of Nature: The Popular Influence of Evolutionary Psychology as a Problem for Sociology'. *Sociology,.41, 917-930*

Kish, V. and Lansdown, R. (2000). Meeting the psychological impact of facial disfigurement ; developing a clinical service for children and families. *Clinical Child Psychology and Psychiatry, 5: 497-511.*

Kleck, R., and Strenta, A. (1980). Perceptions of the impact of negatively valued physical characteristics on social interaction. *Journal of Personality and Social Psychology, 39, 861-873.*

Kleve, L., Rumsey, N., Wyn-Williams, M., and White, P. (2002). The effectiveness of cognitive-behavioural interventions provided by Outlook: a disfigurement support unit. *Journal of Evaluation in Clinical Practice, 8: 387-395.*

Kent, G. (2002).Testing a model of disfigurement: effects of a skin camouflage service on well-being and appearance anxiety. *Psychology and health, vol.17, No. 3, 377-386.*

Kent, G., & Keahone, S. (2001). Social anxiety and disfigurement: The moderating effects of fear of negative evaluation and past experience. *British Journal of Clinical Psychology, 40(1), 23–34.*

Kent, G. (2002). Testing a model of disfigurement: effects of skin a camouflage service on well-being and appearance anxiety. *Psychology and Health, 17, 377–386.*

Kent, G. (2000). Understanding the experiences of people with disfigurements: An integration of four models of social and psychological functioning. *Psychology, Health and Medicine, 5, 117–129.*

Kremer, J., and Schermbrucker, I. (2006).Difference and the psychology of conflict. *The Psychologist, Vol.19, Vol. 3, 160-163.*

Kurzban,R., and Leary, M.R. (2001). Evolutionary origins of stigmatisation: The function of social exclusion. *Psychological Bulletin, 127, 187-202.*

Lansdown, R., Rumsey, N., Bradbury, E., Carr, T. and Partridge, J. (1997). Visibly Different: Coping with Disfigurement. *Oxford: Butterworth-Heinemann.*

Liossi, C.(2003). Appearance related concerns across the general and clinical populations, *City University, London.*

Lochhart, J.S. (1999). Nurses' perception of head and neck oncology patients and surgery: severity of facial disfigurement and patient gender. *Head and Neck Nursing, 17, 12-25.*

McGrouther, D.A. *The last bastion of discrimination. Professor of plastic surgery.*

MacGregor, F.C. (1979). After Plastic Surgery; Adaption and Adjustment. *New York: Praeger.*

MacGregor,F. (1990). Facial disfigurement: Problems and Management of social interaction and implications for mental health. *Aesthetic Plastic Surgery, 14,249-257.*

Moss, T., Rosser, B. (2008). Psychological adjustment to disfigurement. *The psychologist, Vol.21, No.6, 492-495.*

Moss, T. P. (2005). The relationship between objective and subjective ratings of disfigurement severity, and psychological adjustment. *Body Image 2, 151-159.*

Newell, R. (2000). Body image & disfigurement care. *London: Routledge.*

Newell, R., Marks, I. (2000).Phobic nature of social difficulty in facially disfigured people. *British journal of Psychiatry, 176, 177-181.*

Paluck, E.L., and Green, E.P. (2009). Prejudice Reduction: What Works? A Reviewand Assessment of Research and Practice. *Annual Review of Psychology,60,339,367.*

Papadopoulos, L., Bore, R., & Legg, C. (1999). Psychological factors in cutaneous disease: An overview of research. *Psychology, Health and Medicine, 4,107–127..*

Partridge, J., Pearson, A. (2008). 'Don't worry...it's inside that counts'. *The psychologist, Vol. 21, No. 6, 490-491.*

Park, J.H., Faulkner, J. and Schaller, M. (2003). Evolved disease-avoidance processes and contemporary anti-social behaviour and avoidance of people with physical disabilities. *Journal of Non-verbal Behaviour, 27, 65-87.*

Partridge, J. (1996). Facial disfigurement: The full picture. *London: Changing Faces.*

Partridge, J. (1990). The challenge of facial disfigurement. *Changing Faces.*

Rankin, M., Borah, G., Kalick, S. (2005). Perceived functional impact of abnormal facial appearance. *Plastic and reconstructive surgery, 111, 7, 2140-2148.*

Reid, K., Flowers, P., & Larkin, M. (2005). Interpretative phenomenological analysis: An overview and methodological review. *The Psychologist, 18, 20–23.*

Rhodes, G. (2006). The evolutionary psychology of facial beauty. *Annual review of psychology, 57, 199-226.*

Rhodes G, Roberts J, Simmons L.(1999). Reflections on symmetry and attractiveness. *Psychol. Evolution and Gender, 1:279–95*

Richards, H.L., Herrick, A.L., Griffin, K., Gwilliam, P.H.D., and Fortune, D.G. (2004). Psychological adjustment to systemic sclerosis- exploring the association of disease factors, functional ability, body related attitudes and fear of negative evaluation. *Psychology, Health and Medicine, 9, 1, 29-38.*

Roche, D. (2008). The metaphor of facial disfigurement. (*retrieved from* www.huffingtonpost.com/david-roche/***the-metaphor-of-facial****-di_b_144949*.)

Robinson, E., Rumsey, N. and Partridge, J. (1996). An evaluation of the impact of social skills training for facially disfigured people. *British Journal of Plastic Surgery, 49, 281–289.*

Rumsey, N., Bull, R., & Gahagan, D. (1982). The effect of facial disfigurement on the proxemic behaviour of the general public. *Journal of Applied Social Psychology, 12,* 137–150.

Rumsey, N., Bull, R., & Gahagan, D. (1982). A preliminary study of the potential of social skills training for improving the quality of social interaction for the facially disfigured. *Social Behaviour, 1, 143-145.*

Rumsey, N., Clarke, A., and White, P. (2001). Exploring the psychological concerns of outpatients with disfiguring conditions. *Journal of Wound Care, Vol 12, No 7, 247-252.*

Rumsey, N., Clarke, A., White, P., Wyn-Williams, M. And Garlick, W. (2004). Altered body image: appearance-related concerns of people with visible disfigurement. *Journal of Advanced Nursing, 48:443-453.*

Rumsey, N., & D, Harcourt. (2004). Body image and disfigurement: Issues and interventions. *Body Image, 1, 83-97.*

Rumsey, N., & D, Harcourt. (2005). The Psychology of Appearance. *Open University: Maidenhead.*

Rumsey, N. (2004) Psychological aspects of face transplantation: read the small print carefully. *American Journal of Bioethics, 4, 10-13*

Schmid-Ott, G., Burchard, R., Neiderauer, H.H, et al., Stigmatisation experience and quality of life of patients with psoriasis and atopic dermatitis. *Hautartz, 2003, 54, 852-857.*

Shakespeare, T. and Erickson, M. (2000) 'Different Strokes: Beyond Biological Determinism and Social Constructionism' in *Rose, H. and Rose, S. (editors) 'Alas, Poor Darwin: Arguments Against Evolutionary Psychology', Harmony Books, New York*

Smith, J. A., Jarman, M., & Osborn, M. (1999). Doing interpretative phenomenological analysis. *In M. Murray & K. Chamberlain (Eds.), Qualitative health psychology: Theories and methods. London: Sage.*

Smith, J. A. (2008). Qualitative Psychology. *Sage publications Ltd.*

Smith, R.A. (2007). Language of the Lost: An Explication of Stigma Communication. *Communication Theory, 17, 462-483.*

Stevenage, S.V., and Mcay, Y. (1999). Model applicants: The effect of facial appearance on recruitment decisions. *British Journal of Psychology, 90, 221-234.*

Sullivan, R. (2001) Deformity- A modern western prejudice with ancient origins. *Proc R College Physicians Edinburgh, 31, 262-266.*

Tartaglia, A., McMahon, B.T., West, S. L., & Belongia, L. (2005). Workplace discrimination and disfigurement: The national EEOC ADA research project. *Work, 25, 57-65.*

Tebble, N.J., Adams, R., Thomas, D.W., and Patricia, P. (2006). Anxiety and self-consciousness in patients with facial lacerations one week and six months later. *British Journal of Oral and Maxillofacial Surgery, 44, 520-525.*

Thombs, B.D., Notes, L.D., Lawrence, J.W., Magyar-Russell, G., Bresnick, M.G., and

Thompson, A. R., Kent, G., & Smith, J. A. (2002). Living with vitiligo: Dealing with difference. *British Journal of Health Psychology, 7, 213–215.*

Thompson, A. R., & Kent, G. (2001). Adjusting to disfigurement: Processes involved in dealing with being visibly different. *Clinical Psychology Review, 21(5), 663–682.*

Thornhill R, Gangestad SW. 1999. Facial attractiveness. *Trends in Cognitive Sciences. 3:452–60*

Trust, D. (1986). Overcoming Disfigurement: Defeating the problems- physical, social and emotional.

Turner, S., Thomas, P., Dowell, T., Rumsey, N. And Sandy, J. (1997).Psychological outcomes amongst clef patients and their families. *British Journal of Plastic Surgery, 50:1-10.*

Wahl, A.K., Gjengedal, E., and Hanestad, B. R.(2002).The bodily suffering of living with severe psoriasis: In-Depth Interviews with hospitalised Patients with Psoriasis. *Qualitative Health Research, Vol 12, No 2, 250-261.*

Wardle, C., and T, Boyce. (2009). Media coverage and audience reception of disfigurement on television. *The Healing Foundation. (retrieved from a link at http://www.changingfaces.org.uk/show/feature/News-portrayals-of-disfigurement.)*

Willig, C. (2008). Introducing Qualitative Research in Psychology. *Second Edition, McGraw- Hill Education.*

Ye, E. (1998). Psychological morbidity in patients with facial and neck burns. *Burns 24, 646-648.*

Appendix 1

Interview schedule

- Given them the information sheet.
- Explain the rational for the interview being recorded and obtain permission.
- Explain they do not have to answer any questions they are uncomfortable with.
- Allow time for any questions to be asked.
- Obtain a signed consent form.

Interview (part one)

1. Describe a definition of facial disfigurement.

2. Could you tell what you believe to be some of the causes of facial disfigurement?

3. What do you think about facial disfigurement?

4. If you had to describe what facial disfigurement means to you what would you say?
    - Prompt- What comes to your mind?
    - What images?
    - How would you define it?

5. What is your experience of facial difference?
    - Could you tell me a more about it?
    - How was the experience for you? How did you find it? Did it affect you in any way?
    - What did the experience mean to you?

Interview(part two) with the use of three images.

6. What are your thought on this face?

- Prompts- What do you notice? Any associations? How do you see this person?

7. How do you think you would feel seeing this person on the street or being introduced to them?

8. How did you find the experience of looking at the faces?
9. Do you have anything else you would like to add/ask?

Appendix 2

Consent Form

An exploration of views and perceptions of facial disfigurement

I have read and understood the information sheet and this consent form. I have had an opportunity to ask questions about my participation.

I understand that I am under no obligation to take part in this study.

By completing the following I understand that I am participating in a research study and the data I provide may be published. I understand that the researcher will not use my name in any publication and will endeavour to protect my anonymity.

I understand that I have the right to withdraw from this study at any stage without giving any reason.

I agree to participate in this study.

Name of participant: _____

Age :   _____

Gender: _____

Signature of participant: _____

Signature of researcher: _____

Date: _____

Contact details of the researcher

Name of researcher: Sophie Tolmie

Address: Undergraduate psychology Student, School of Social Sciences, media and communication.
Queen Margaret University

Edinburgh EH21 6UU

Email / Telephone: 06004308@qmu.ac.uk

Contact details of my project supervisor

Name of supervisor: Dr Zoe Chouliara

Address: Psychology

School of Social Sciences, Media and Communication.

Queen Margaret University

Edinburgh EH21 6UU

Email : zchouliara@qmu.ac.uk

Contact details of my independent advisor

Name of advisor: Dr Stuart Wilson

Address: Psychology

School of Social Sciences, Media and Communication.

Queen Margaret University

Edinburgh EH21 6UU

Email : swilson@qmu.ac.uk

Appendix 3

Information Sheet

Exploring views and perceptions of facial disfigurement

My name is Sophie Tolmie and I am an undergraduate student from the School of Psychology at Queen Margaret University in Edinburgh. As part of my degree course, I am undertaking a research project for my honours dissertation. This project is exploring public views, perceptions and experiences of facial disfigurement . Facial disfigurement can be described as 'a difference from a culturally defined norm which is visible to others' . I am looking for volunteers to participate in the project. There are no criteria; everyone is welcome to take part.

If you agree to participate in the study, you will be asked to take part in an interview that will last approximately 30 minutes. In this interview you will be asked a series of questions on what you feel about the topic of facial difference. With your permission, the interview will be audio taped. If you are not comfortable with this please tell me and I will take notes instead. It should be noted that I will use images of facial difference in my interviews. The researcher is not aware of any risks associated with the use of these images. You will be free to withdraw from the study at any stage, and you do not have to give a reason.

All discussion that takes place during the interview will remain completely confidential. Any audiotape recordings of the interview will be destroyed on completion of the research. Your name will be replaced with a participant number, and it will not be possible for you to be identified in any reporting of the data gathered.

If you have read and understood this information sheet, any questions you had have been answered, and you would like to be a participant in the study, please now sign the consent form. Please note that even after you have signed the consent form you are still free to leave the research/interview at any point.

If you would like to speak to some else about this project you can contact my independent advisor Stuart Wilson (contact details at the bottom).

Contact details of the researcher

Name of researcher: Sophie Tolmie

Address: Undergraduate psychology Student, School of Social Sciences,

　　　　　media and communication

　　　　　Queen Margaret University

　　　　　Edinburgh EH21 6UU

Email / Telephone: 06004308@qmu.ac.uk

Contact details of my project supervisor

Name of adviser: Dr Zoe Chouliara

Address: Psychology

　　　　　School of Social Sciences, Media and Communication.

　　　　　Queen Margaret University

　　　　　Edinburgh EH21 6UU

Email : zchouliara@qmu.ac.uk

Contact details of my independent advisor

Name of advisor: Dr Stuart Wilson

Address: Psychology

　　　　　School of Social Sciences, Media and Communication.

　　　　　Queen Margaret University

　　　　　Edinburgh EH21 6UU

Email : swilson@qmu.ac.uk

Appendix 4

Debriefing form

I would like to thank you for taking part in my research project. This study has aimed to explore public perceptions, views and experiences of facial disfigurement.

This project has aimed to explore the perceptions and experiences of facial difference in the general public , as research into the area of facial difference, has found that people who display a facial disfigurement often experience discrimination (Tartagila et al, 2005; Rumsey et al,1982), prejudice, unwanted comments ,questions, stares, and stares. In addition, the public often display ignorance towards the nature of their facial disfigurement (Macgregor, 1979; Van Der Donk et al, 1994). The aim of this study was to explore how the public feel, view and what they believe about facial disfigurement.

Please note that the interview that you have taken part in is completely non judgmental, and the data will not be used in a way to judge your views and experiences.

I would like to thank you again, for taking the time to participate in my study, it is very much appreciated.

If you have any questions at all please do not hesitate to contact me at 06004308@qmu.ac.uk.

Information on my completed project will be made available to all participants if they wish.

For more information on the topic of facial difference please visit;
http://www.changingfaces.org.uk/Home.

Appendix 5 -(images 1-3)

Image 1

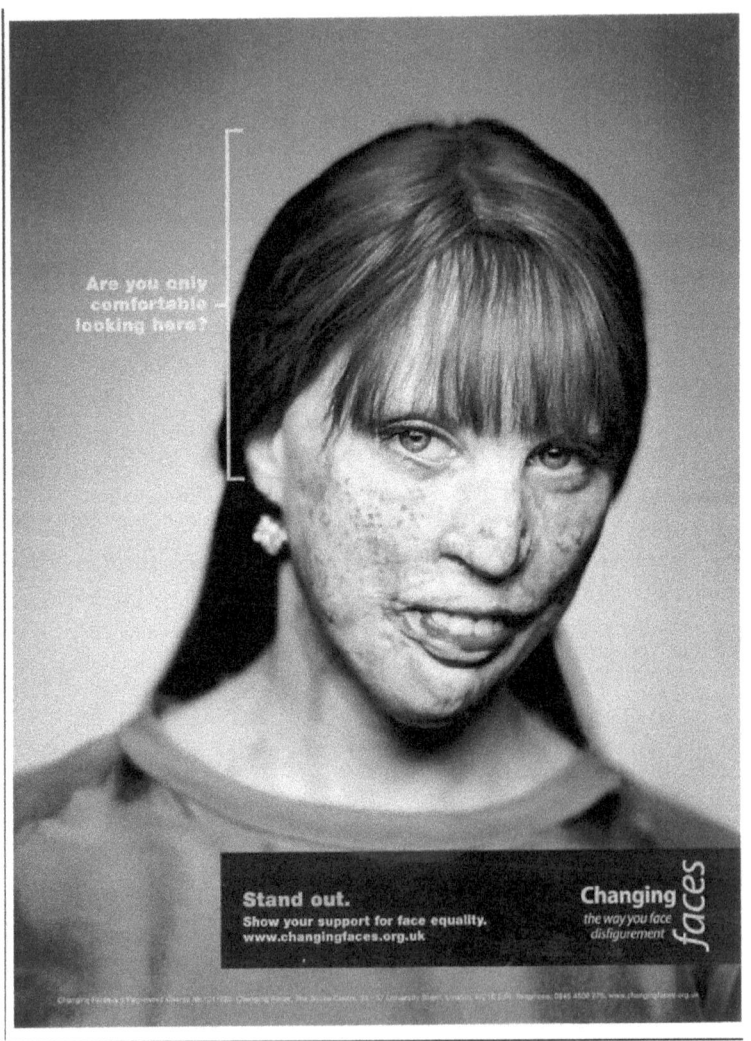

Image 2

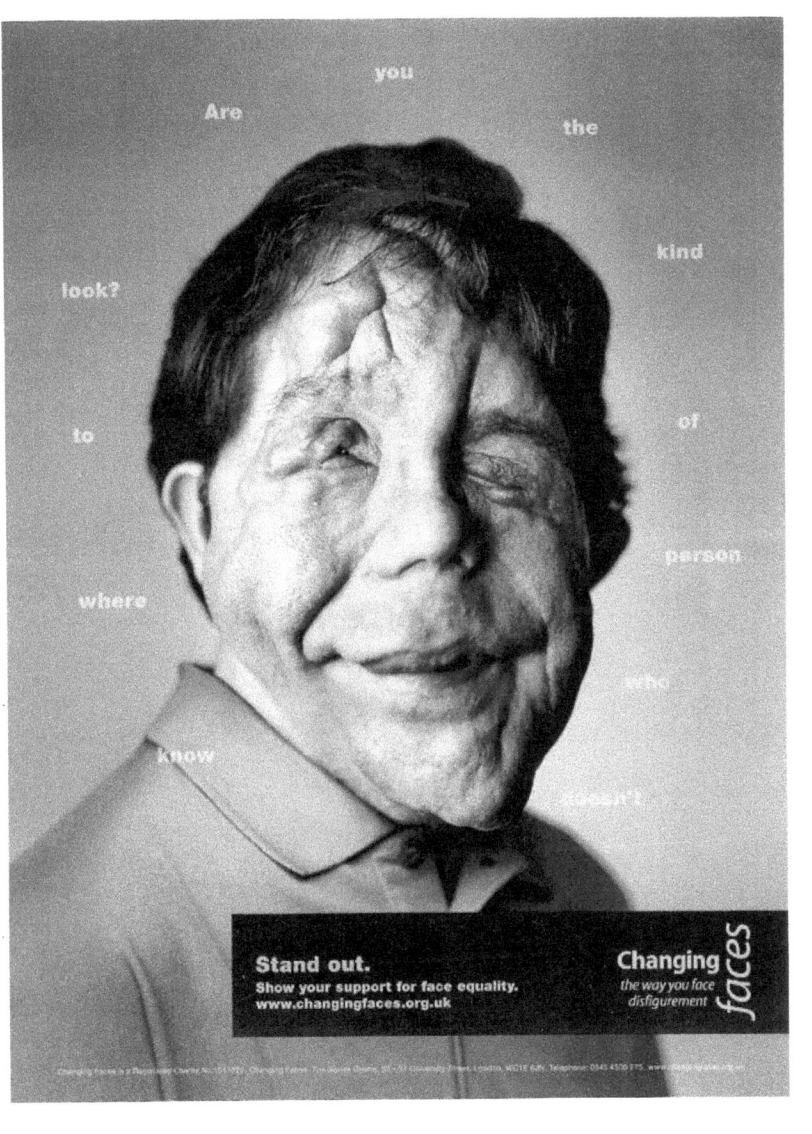

Image 3

VDM publishing house ltd.

Scientific Publishing House
offers
free of charge publication

of current academic research papers, Bachelor´s Theses, Master's Theses, Dissertations or Scientific Monographs

If you have written a thesis which satisfies high content as well as formal demands, and you are interested in a remunerated publication of your work, please send an e-mail with some initial information about yourself and your work to *info@vdm-publishing-house.com*.

Our editorial office will get in touch with you shortly.

VDM Publishing House Ltd.
Meldrum Court 17.
Beau Bassin
Mauritius
www.vdm-publishing-house.com

Lightning Source UK Ltd.
Milton Keynes UK
UKHW010926071118
331889UK00001B/156/P